Contents

Ambushed by History:
  Introduction by Elizabeth Schafer   *vii*

JUMP FOR JORDAN

  Part One   1

  Part Two   16

  Part Three   33

  Part Four   43

  Part Five   49

Currency Press acknowledges the Traditional Owners of the Country on which we live and work. We pay our respects to all Aboriginal and Torres Strait Islander Elders, past and present.

Sal Sharah as Sahir and Doris Younane as Mara in Griffin Theatre Company's 2014 production. (Photo: Brett Boardman)

Ambushed by History

Jump for Jordan is a shimmering, shifting kaleidoscope of a play. It offers fragments of character, splashes of narrative, glimpses of family history, plus plenty of generational conflict and sibling rivalry. The play reflects on the experience of leaving home – as a migrant, as a refugee, as an aspiring archaeologist, as a twenty-year-old, as a lesbian. It is funny, but also moving, and it asks audiences to consider seeing things a little differently: shifting their point of view, asking questions about prejudices, turning some light on blind spots.

At the centre of this Sydney play is a family with its roots in Jordan and Palestine. At a time when, for many, this area of the world is primarily associated with conflict, the plight of refugees, and the tactical deployment of terror, *Jump for Jordan* invites us to rethink. Jordan is a cradle of civilisation, Petra an archaeological treasure house, Amman a sophisticated city. While Jordan is, as Sophie's father Sahir tells us, 'the most invaded place on earth', its namesake river winds its way through the sacred texts of three world religions – Christianity, Islam and Judaism.

By contrast, in the fears and fantasies of Sophie, the central character in *Jump for Jordan*, her mother's country is a place where unwilling brides can be bundled into marriage. The news that her Aunt Azza is to visit Australia unleashes Sophie's unease, even her nightmares, in relation to her cultural heritage. Avenging Azza is the result, a caricature that plays to every negative stereotype of Arab-woman-as-cultural-policewoman. As a comic Fury, Avenging Azza produces a magic carpet in order to whisk Sophie off to force her to marry 'Hairy Toothless Tarek'. But in reality, Azza is an educated, compassionate woman, concerned about her nieces and demanding of her sister Mara: 'Why are your daughters so miserable?'

One reason Sophie finds it hard to connect with the real Azza is because Sophie can only communicate with her by means of Mara. Because Sophie cannot speak Arabic and Azza cannot speak English, the bi-lingual Mara is in complete control, translating and mistranslating to create the meanings and the histories she desires. *Jump for Jordan* is theatrically ambitious its representation of different levels of language competence by means of different accents and fluency. So Azza speaks fluent English when in the storyline she is speaking Arabic. When Azza tries to speak English it is heavily accented and broken. This device keeps the audience on their toes but what is very clear is that, by the end of the play, Sophie and Azza are managing to reach out to each other. Sophie is beginning to learn Arabic, and, in stilted English, Azza has told something of the story of Layla – Sophie's other aunt, who was Sahir's sister and Azza's dear friend and fellow teacher. Azza remarks on how closely Sophie resembles Layla physically, invoking another kind of 'archaeology', that of genes and heritage on a biological and physiological level. And when Sophie's partner Sam conducts an archaeological analysis of the battered copy of *Alice in Wonderland* that once belonged to Layla, this begins to open another door for Sophie. As Azza explains in her broken English, Layla valued the book because 'Alice think free'. Perhaps Sophie will also soon be able to begin to 'think free'.

Jump for Jordan reminds us that we only know our nearest and dearest in part; we don't fully understand the journeys our parents made, and we won't fully understand the journeys our children are making. We can only excavate, like the aspiring archaeologists Sophie and Sam. We can get out our trowels, uncover the artefacts, look at the photographs, but how do we know we are not misreading what we see? Sophie knows her dad was from Palestine but has no idea why he fled to Australia:

> He escaped or something. Walked north to Lebanon.

Mara has buried the family trauma that brought Sahir to Australia. She has covered it with layers of lies and false appearances, trapped by her expatriate – and dangerously nostalgic – memory of an Amman and a Jordan that have moved on. After Sahir's death, Mara is the gatekeeper of family knowledge until Azza arrives and encourages Sophie to excavate.

Jump for Jordan has five women at its centre: Sophie, her sister Loren, her mother Mara, her aunt Azza, and her partner Sam. All are affected by what happened to another woman, Layla. Focusing on women in this way is still not that common in mainstream theatre. *Jump for Jordan* is also unorthodox in the dramaturgy the play offers: slivers, impressions, history intermingled with the present, facts alongside fantasies, science alongside dreams, desires alongside archaeology. The play presents a dramatic quicksand and the audience won't be able to grasp hold of everything they want to excavate. When did Sophie's gentle dad, Sahir, die? Will Sophie conquer Arabic? Or will she give up as she has done with so many university courses? And will Mara and Sophie ever manage to talk without rowing?

When Azza tells her sister Mara, 'You were ambushed by history. Most people are,' she is trying to galvanise Mara to stop feeling self-pity. But, of course, everyone gets caught up in, if not ambushed by, history. Some, like Mara and her family, are ambushed by the big events of history – world affairs, wars, terrorism. Sahir fled for his life and Mara followed reluctantly, abandoning the home she loved. Meanwhile others struggle with the pressures of local or family history and are ambushed by unexpected illness or death. But the play itself has also been ambushed by history. When Sam asked Sophie 'Would you marry me? Would you?' in the first production in 2014, the postal survey on same-sex marriage was still three years in the future. I am writing this just one week after Australia voted yes. I hope Sophie is jumping for joy.

Elizabeth Schafer
November 2017
Elizabeth Schafer is Professor of Drama and Theatre Studies
at Royal Holloway, University of London.

Anna Houston as Sam and Alice Ansara as Sophie in Griffin Theatre Company's 2014 production. (Photo: Brett Boardman)

Jump for Jordan was first produced by Griffin Theatre Company at SBW Stables Theatre, Sydney, on 14 February 2014, with the following cast:

SOPHIE	Alice Ansara
SAM	Anna Houston
LOREN	Sheridan Harbridge
MARA	Doris Younane
SAHIR	Sal Sharah
AZZA	Camilla Ah Kin

Director, Iain Sinclair
Designer, Pip Runciman
Lighting Designer, Nicholas Rayment
Composer & Sound Designer, Nate Edmondson
Dramaturg, Jennifer Medway
Stage Manager, Edwina Guinness

PRODUCTION NOTES

Like the strata of occupation in a disturbed archaeological dig site, the scenes in this play are often constructed of layers of narrative that collapse in on each other. A sequential reading is interrupted, and only fragments of what happened are offered. Attention must be on context as well as content. The borders between scenes are intended to be porous.

LANGUAGE NOTES

Jump For Jordan is a bi-lingual play written almost entirely in English. Generally, when characters speak in their first language, the syntax is complex; when they speak in their second language, the syntax is simple. In the first production, accents were also used to denote first and second language. When characters spoke in their first language, actors used Australian accents; when characters spoke in their second language, actors used Arabic accents, and sometimes converted verbs to the present simple tense. Being a product of Sophia's imagination, and a caricature, Avenging Azza is an exception; her language is complex, and in production, was heavily accented in Arabic. Clarity in the bi-lingual scenes depends on knowing to whom each line is directed.

CHARACTERS

SOPHIE, a would-be archaeologist

SAM / STUDENT SAM / TRUCKIE SAM, partner

LOREN, sister

MARA / YOUNG MARA, mother, from Jordan

SAHIR / YOUNG SAHIR, father, from Palestine

AZZA / AVENGING AZZA, aunt, from Jordan

'Multiple' characters (e.g. MARA / YOUNG MARA) are different iterations that are either real, remembered, or imagined by Sophie. All iterations of a character are to be played by the same actor. Six actors are required in total.

SETTING

The play is set in Sydney's West and Inner West. More broadly, it is set in Sophie's fluctuating levels of consciousness: reality, memory, gleaned family history, anxious projection, and insomnia-induced conversations with the dead.

PART ONE

1.

Present: Flat. SOPHIE *rifles through clothes.*

Past: House. MARA *yells at* LOREN.

Past: Sophie's workplace. LOREN *yells at* SOPHIE.

LOREN: Mum was shattered when you left.

MARA: Why didn't you talk to her? Why didn't you find out?

LOREN: No warning. Just pissed off and dumped me in the shit.

MARA: Sisters tells sisters everything!

LOREN: Not one fight with Mum that week. Should've guessed.

MARA: You knew. You helped her.

LOREN: I copped it big time.

MARA: Weren't a good enough sister.

LOREN: Her guilt and crap.

MARA: No phone number, no address, she could be dead in Kings Cross!

LOREN: Drama queen!

MARA: How could she do this?

LOREN: Run away at twenty-one! Shit, Sophie, no-one does that.

MARA: Books in a taxi! Bras in the gutter! Neighbours saw everything!

SAM: Sophie.

SOPHIE: What?

MARA: You stupid

LOREN: impulsive

MARA: unmarried

LOREN: brat!

A jet screams overhead.

2.

Imagination: Airport. Customs. AVENGING AZZA *enters.*

VOICEOVER: Welcome to Australia, land of drought and sweeping drama
   queens. Anything to declare?

AVENGING AZZA *opens her bag and declares various weapons.*

Thank you. Enjoy your stay.

AVENGING AZZA *nods and exits.*

3.

Recent past: House. SOPHIE *is at the front door.*

SOPHIE: Mum. Do you have cancer?

MARA: No.

SOPHIE: Are you sick?

MARA: No.

SOPHIE: So, why the frantic call from Loren? *Sophie, get your arse over here now?*

MARA: Loren doesn't swear.

SOPHIE: Does *she* have cancer?

MARA: No.

SOPHIE: She said the word *emergency.* I was literally imagining the worst on the train. Pussy sores, oxygen tanks.

MARA: There's a wedding.

SOPHIE: Oh.

MARA: My second daughter is marrying first.

SOPHIE: She could've mentioned it.

MARA: The look on their faces.

SOPHIE: What are you talking about?

MARA: Vince's parents.

SOPHIE: Vince is the groom?

MARA: I told them. They couldn't believe it. *My eldest daughter, I don't know where she lives!*

SOPHIE: You *do* know.

MARA: For months I didn't.

SOPHIE: And for three years, you totally disowned me. For the last three years, you acted like I didn't exist.

MARA: Azza is coming.

SOPHIE: Who?

MARA: Your aunt.

SOPHIE: When?

MARA: Next month. *I'm coming to the wedding, pick me up, I'll be there on the sixth.* As if she's my boss.

SOPHIE: Aunty Azza?

MARA: Fifteen years no contact. Then she smells a wedding. Can't fly here quick enough.

SOPHIE: She did make contact. She sent cards, remember, which you wouldn't let us open.

MARA: Sophia. In Jordan, you could have been killed. Had your ears cut off for not listening.

4.

Present: Flat. SAM *checks on* SOPHIE *who is rifling through clothes.*

SAM: Sophie.

SOPHIE: What?

SAM: Have you slept yet?

SOPHIE: Do you think Mum'll tell her? She'll tell her. She's her sister. She has every right to tell her sister what happened.

SAM: It's three a.m.

SOPHIE: What if right now they're sobbing in my bedroom? If Azza and Mum are having this completely extreme empathy session? Which honestly, that's fine, it's their moment.

SAM: Come to bed.

SOPHIE: Azza would've got through customs, would've seen Mum at the gate with just Loren, not me, and she would've spent the whole car trip home going, *Where's Sophie?* And Mum would've been like, *Don't worry, we'll talk about it later.* Try to sway her from thinking, *Where's Sophie?* with stupid crap questions like, *Are you good? Was the flight good? Was the weather good when you left Amman?*

SAM: I'm turning the light off.

SOPHIE: I'm so gonna get pelted. *Why'd you run away? Why don't you have a husband? Why are you such a brat?*

SAM: You're not a brat.

SOPHIE: Not specifically, but—

SAM: You're overexcited.

SOPHIE: And my aunt's nearly sixty. She'll be stuck in the Dark Ages, probably.

SAM: Sophie, you're totally up for this. We've devised a plan. Gone through the whole meeting process.

SOPHIE: Yep. Right. Chill.

SAM: Keep it low-key. Don't get provoked.

SOPHIE: But what if it gets out-of-hand emotional?

SAM: You lower your voice. You count to three, and say...?

SOPHIE: *Okay, I have to go, I'll call you tomorrow.*

SAM: Koala stamp. Goodnight.

SOPHIE: But, Sam, she's my aunty. I was in school when I last saw her, primary school, I was like ten.

SAM: Well, in that case, just spew your guts up. Guilt trips, tantrum attacks, not part of the plan, but I'm pretty sure you can handle it.

SOPHIE: Really?

SAM: No.

SOPHIE: Okay. You're right. Thanks, Sam. I'm on it.

5.

Recent past: House. SOPHIE *is at the front door.*

MARA: The wedding. You have to come. Loren wants family. Azza will expect you.

SOPHIE: Does she know I ran away?

MARA: No.

SOPHIE: Will you tell her?

MARA: Will you move back home?

SOPHIE: I knew you'd—

MARA: Come home. Sleep here. I can measure you as I sew. Not have to unpick each time you visit.

SOPHIE: Unpick?

MARA: Your dress. You're one of five bridesmaids. We dropped one to make room for you.

SOPHIE: Bet *that* went down well.

MARA: Not interested? Okay. Go.

SOPHIE: Wait. I'm a bridesmaid?

MARA: Yes.

SOPHIE: What are the dresses like?

MARA: Off-the-shoulder, pleated bodice, cocktail length, in emerald.

SOPHIE: That's hotter than I expected.

MARA: Vince's sisters, all beautiful, all the same size. But you, look at you. Thick legs, long waist, no bust. I'll have to mix up three sizes to make your dress fit properly.

SOPHIE: Primmed-up and pretty. Good luck.

MARA: Too hard? No problem. Leave.

SOPHIE: Mum—

MARA: Three more years, go.

SOPHIE: All I meant was, I'm not super girlie, or good in heels, I'll just—

MARA: You can pick your own shoes.

SOPHIE: Really?

MARA: They have to be black.

SOPHIE: Fine… Do you really want me in the bridal party in front of potential relatives?

MARA: … Yes.

SOPHIE: Mainly because of Azza, right?

MARA: And Loren.

SOPHIE: And afterwards?

MARA: You can keep the dress.

SOPHIE: Oh.

MARA: And maybe…

SOPHIE: Come for Christmas?

MARA: Let's do the wedding first.

> MARA *exits.*

> *Imagination:* SAHIR *enters.*

SAHIR: Jordan means *the one who descends.*

SOPHIE: Dad?

> SAHIR *walks.* SOPHIE *follows.*

6.

Imagination: SAHIR *and* SOPHIE *walk.*

SAHIR: I bought the highest block of land. A quarter acre on top of the hill. I walked from Campbelltown station. The road was brand new. Sticky with bitumen and still without street lights. When I found the display home, I sat on the front step. Other people arrived with sleeping bags and sandwiches, but I was the first.

SOPHIE: Dad, did you ever have insomnia? It feels like withdrawals, but I don't know from what? If it hits 3 a.m. and I'm still awake, I go for a walk like we used to. And I think of you walking out of the lowest depression on earth. Up through the Rift Valley, treading on artefacts, probably, I so wanted to discover.

SAHIR: I stayed awake all night. When the saleslady came in the morning, I signed the contract, gave her a cheque for all the money we had. Then I ran through paddocks of grabbing grass up to our block on the top of the hill. The wind was strong. My clothes were like whips.

7.

Present: Flat. SOPHIE *is still rifling through clothes.*

Past: House. MARA *yells at* LOREN.

Past: Sophie's workplace. LOREN *yells at* SOPHIE.

MARA: Ring someone! Where is she? Who is she with?

SOPHIE: Sam?

LOREN: You're a complete dick.

MARA: In the street like a bag lady!

LOREN: What the fuck were you thinking?

SOPHIE: You awake?

LOREN: You've left me with Mum. One on one. That sucks.

MARA: I wanted children who would not shame me like this!

LOREN: Did it feel liberating shoving your life into garbage bags?

MARA: Treating my trust like rubbish!

LOREN: You left knickers on the lawn. We had to pick them up with tongs.

MARA: Unforgivable.

LOREN: This is the dumbest fucking thing you've ever done.

SOPHIE: Sam?

MARA: From this minute, my disgraceful daughter does not exist.

SOPHIE: I think I'm having a panic attack.

A jet screams overhead.

8.

Recent past: House. SOPHIE *steps back into her family home.*

MARA: I should measure you. For the dress.

She grabs a tape measure and starts measuring.

Stand there... Stand still... Move home.

SOPHIE: Mum—

MARA: Your room is all ready. Like you never left in front of the whole street with no husband.

SOPHIE: Please don't—

MARA: If you move home, you can sleep in all morning. Sip coffee on the patio with Azza who is old now, older than me, maybe even dead soon, and you'll never see her again.

SOPHIE: Mum.

MARA: Then I have to tell her. *Azza, Sophia left home, lives with strangers, left neighbours shaking their heads, too disgusted to talk to me.*

SOPHIE: Mum, I'll visit Aunty every day if you want... but forcing me back home, I'm sorry, it's off the table.

MARA: One month.

SOPHIE: No.

MARA: .

SOPHIE: Aunty obviously will want to know why, so, how about... whatever story makes it less terrible, I'll back you up, okay? Just tell me what you want me to say.

Pause.

MARA: Okay, say... you left home with no husband... to study. Your university was far away. Your classes were at night. Trains to Campbelltown are full of dangerous rapists. Say that.

SOPHIE: Okay.

MARA: And this flatmate person you live with.

SOPHIE: Samantha.

MARA: Samira. You met her at church. You go to church. Never miss. You watch romantic movies. Plan weddings and practise hairdos.

SOPHIE: Clearly.

MARA: And you work at the museum.

SOPHIE: I actually don't even have my degree yet.

MARA: What?

SOPHIE: I've repeated some subjects. I'm doing my last one.

MARA: Don't say that! Say you work at the museum. Your job is important.

SOPHIE: Can we lie about me as little as possible?

MARA: Your job is impressive... but at night. The trains are still full of dangerous rapists, so you must live in the city to be safe.

SOPHIE: Mum, I sell gold pens to manicured barristers at David Jones.

MARA: Sophia, your aunt teaches at the best school in Amman.

SOPHIE: And *you* didn't even teach us Arabic!

> *Pause.*

MARA: Remember in Jordan when a man in the traffic was rude to Azza?

> *Imagination:* AVENGING AZZA *enters.*

AVENGING AZZA: Peak hour. He was driving like a maniac. *Lanes? What lanes?* He swerved. Cut in front. Cut me off. I pulled him out of the car by the neck. I threw this public enemy infidel onto his knees and delivered a disciplinary beating!

SOPHIE: I don't remember—

AVENGING AZZA: If someone does wrong, I teach them a lesson. This is normal for me, Sophia. A day-to-day activity.

> *Imagination:* AVENGING AZZA *exits.*

SOPHIE: Mum, leaving home, in Australia, it's what people do.

MARA: In Jordan, the law would let us tie you up and drop you down a well.

SOPHIE: .

MARA: You're an odd shape, Sophia. I hope I have enough fabric.

> MARA *exits.*

9.

> *Present: Flat.* SOPHIE *dresses to meet* AZZA. SAM *packs a bag to take to university.*

SOPHIE: What if my aunt slams the door in my face? Turns her back on me? Oh God, if she does that, I'll completely—

SAM: Sophie, I know you think this, but you're not the source of all evil.

SOPHIE: I ran away.

SAM: You left home when you were twenty-one.

SOPHIE: I literally fled.

SAM: Years ago. Ancient history, babe.

SOPHIE: It's not. It still hurts Mum. It's the first thing she'll blurt out all over Azza. And Azza, I bet she's horrified, sharpening knives—

SAM: Japanese ones are the best, apparently.

SOPHIE: Sam, I'm totally right about this.

SAM: You are totally talking shit. What you're freaking out about is based on—

SOPHIE: Experience.

SAM: Not recent experience.

SOPHIE: No, but—

SAM: Could you recognise your aunt in a crowd?

SOPHIE: … If I studied the noses I might—

SAM: You don't know her at all. So don't go there expecting some kind of slut-shaming hate-fest. It could be really cool. Arms flung around poor prodigal daughter. Knives turned into tuning forks. Cue music.

SOPHIE: That won't happen.

SAM: Your mum broke three years of silence. Your aunt's flown in from Jordan. How is that not promising?

SOPHIE: But—

SAM: It's just a visit. Stick to what we rehearsed. Leave the rest in the lap of the goddess.

SOPHIE: Okay.

SAM *is packed and ready to head out the door.*

Wait. How do I look? Ironically retro and self-aware?

SAM: Amish.

SOPHIE: Hey, remember how I used to dress?

SAM: Punk lite.

SOPHIE: Indi-goth, but I kind of regret it now, rejecting Mum's stupid wog view of women like that. She was strict, but she never pushed me into an arranged marriage or anything.

SAM: You were free to find me.

SOPHIE: A chick who lived in her lab coat.

SAM: You complaining?

SOPHIE: I'm remembering… particles of dust on your eyelashes.

SAM: Dust from all the places we'll go to next year. Troy, Ephesus, Petra—

SOPHIE: If I'm not killed.

SAM: Bored now. 'Bye.

SOPHIE: Where are you going?

SAM *holds up her assignment.*

Oh my God, your last assignment. Sam, that's awesome. I forgot.

SAM: I know.

SOPHIE: You'll have two degrees. Two in the time I took to do one.

SAM: Good luck. I'll call you.

SOPHIE: Thanks. You've been amazing. Have you got 50 bucks?

SAM: ?

SOPHIE: Twenty?

SAM: ?

SOPHIE: Train fare?

SAM: Are you broke?

SOPHIE: No.

SAM: You can't be broke.

SOPHIE: I'm not.

SAM: You've been saving up.

SOPHIE: I have, for our big trip, which is absolutely on the cards next year.

SAM: Did you go shopping?

SOPHIE: My face, Sam, my skin! Seriously, I'm breaking out really badly. I just needed some Clarins.

SAM: What else?

SOPHIE: Nothing. Some clothes. New boots. Loren's wedding present. A present for Aunty. That's all. Make-up. That's all. Special shampoo so my hair doesn't frizz—

SAM: Make-up?

SOPHIE: But I've got textbooks. Herodotus. I'll get through my last subject, go to Gould's Bookshop after the wedding and sell them and pay you straight back.

SAM: Credit cards?

SOPHIE: Maxed out.

SAM: Right.

SOPHIE: But we're totally still going to Petra. I'll save up and be binge-free, I promise, but right now, it's like I'm about to travel back to where my family come from, and I want them to look at me and feel proud of me and not harass me or be ashamed.

SAM: I'm sorry, but that frock is stupid.

SOPHIE: I know.

Pause.

SAM: Your guilt needs its own bedroom.

SOPHIE: I know.

Pause.

SAM: Every single Christmas… you're crushed.

SOPHIE: Yes. And if I'm disowned again, I don't think I'll cope.

SAM *gives* SOPHIE *some money.*

As soon as I get paid, I'll—

SAM: It'll be brilliant, Sophie, it'll be epic.

SOPHIE: Will it?

SAM: Yes. Except for the bit about Herodotus. You've already sold your copy. Flog *my* copy, and you *will* be killed, okay?

SAM *exits.*

10.

Present: Garage. SOPHIE *finds* LOREN *smoking in Sahir's car.*

SOPHIE: Loren.

LOREN: Shit!

LOREN *stashes the cigarettes in the glovebox, then realises it's* SOPHIE.

SOPHIE: Does Mum know you smoke?

LOREN: Trust you to sneak up.

She lights up again.

Did you walk?

SOPHIE: Walk?

LOREN: From the station. You were supposed to call. You were supposed to be picked up. I picked Aunt Azza up. I do all the driving. I drive Mum to Liverpool to shop so no-one here sees her and asks *where's Sophia?*

SOPHIE: Did she tell Aunty about me?

LOREN: You're *so* gonna cop it. They sobbed all night because of you. Heavy-duty hysterical.

SOPHIE: I knew it.

LOREN: It's like SBS in there. No English. Can't understand a word.

SOPHIE: How's Aunty?

LOREN: She comes out of customs, and Mum transforms. Ultra Arab. One minute she's cooking Vince steak and chips, next thing she's asking me where to buy goat. Vince won't eat goat.

SOPHIE: What'd she say?

LOREN: I put biscuits out. Mum lost it. Said Arabs use this special order when they serve visitors.

SOPHIE: They do?

LOREN: Food's food. Who cares?

SOPHIE: Maybe we do. With visitors, didn't Mum—?

LOREN: Visitors? Mum cut ties, Sophia. She doesn't go out now. Not even to bingo. Invited no-one to the wedding. Vince's extended family is coming. A whole village from Italy.

SOPHIE: Aunt Azza's here.

LOREN: She's a gatecrasher. And you're a deliberately difficult self-centred brat. You left me in the firing line. You owe me, Sophia. Big time.

Imagination: SAHIR *enters.*

SAHIR: The Jordan depression is a unique geographical feature.

SOPHIE: Dad?

SAHIR *walks.* SOPHIE *follows him.*

11.

Imagination: SOPHIE *walks with* SAHIR.

Past: YOUNG MARA *enters holding a bunch of native flowers.*

SAHIR: I picked your mum up from the airport. I kissed her for the first time in two years, then gave her a bunch of flowers I'd grown myself. We took the train, then walked for ages to our hilltop block of land. The footpaths were still clumps of clay, so we took our time, counting cows, jumping over ditches.

Past: YOUNG MARA *surveys the location of her new home.*

Mara, look. Those trees left standing together, they're called iron barks. They're putting a park there... This is called kangaroo grass, it flowers at Christmas... and this, this is where our front door will be...
to our children-to-be
to your home with me
peace

Past: YOUNG MARA *glares at* SAHIR.

Darling, take your shoes off. Land in this land with me.

Past: YOUNG MARA *is appalled. She drops the flowers and exits.*

SOPHIE: Once you landed here, you only looked forward. So why am I always looking back?

SAHIR: Jordan is the most invaded place on earth.

SOPHIE: I wish you weren't dead.

SAHIR *exits.*

12.

Past: University. STUDENT SAM *enters wearing a lab coat.*

STUDENT SAM: When did you go to Jordan?

SOPHIE: I was ten. My first big trip. My only big trip.

STUDENT SAM: Why Jordan?

SOPHIE: Mum's from there. Dad's from Palestine. He escaped or something. Walked north to Lebanon.

STUDENT SAM: Tell me everything you remember.

SOPHIE: ... Me crying because Dad wouldn't come with us... Mum getting upset at every place she took us. Mum and my aunty having this massive fight...

STUDENT SAM: Intense.

SOPHIE: Yeah.

STUDENT SAM: What else?

SOPHIE: No Dead Sea, no Red Sea, no camel ride.

STUDENT SAM: Good memories? You must have some.

SOPHIE: How my aunt held my hand as she showed us her school… Hookah pipes in cafés and how really weird that looked. Me and my sister flying kites up on the Citadel.

STUDENT SAM: You just saw Amman?

SOPHIE: Mainly, but we did drive to this ruin where fake gladiators whacked the shit out of each other.

STUDENT SAM: Did you get to Petra?

SOPHIE: I wish.

STUDENT SAM: I'd love to go. Twist between cliffs and outrun the flash floods.

SOPHIE: I'm definitely going. But, God, the cost. You know Courtney?

STUDENT SAM: That North Shore glamazon?

SOPHIE: Yes. She went on the Pella dig. Four grand gone in three weeks. Pennies from her inheritance. But I totally have to go.

STUDENT SAM: Out of the lab and the library, into the field—

SOPHIE: Actually excavating.

STUDENT SAM: Touching what we've studied.

SOPHIE: Feeling the harsh sun heating everything up.

STUDENT SAM: If we woke up there, we'd see the temples flush.

SOPHIE: Would we?

STUDENT SAM: When the first flash of sun hits them, apparently they flush and look like they're moving.

SOPHIE: I'd love to go.

STUDENT SAM: We could go for coffee. Discuss the desert over dessert.

SOPHIE: If I could walk on the land Mum and Dad came from, I might discover deeper connections…

STUDENT SAM: Canoodle over some strudel?

SOPHIE: … or unearth unthinkable things that… [*Registering* STUDENT SAM'*s comment*] What?

13.

Present: Garage. LOREN *smokes in Sahir's car.*

LOREN: Fuck I hate this car. No airbags. Vince's dad drives a burgundy

Merc. His brother knows this bloke. Insurance jobs. He offered to
torch it.

SOPHIE: Dad's car?

LOREN: Four grand, Mum would've got. She couldn't pay for anything.

SOPHIE: Mum made the bridesmaids' dresses, Loren, she bought all the
fabric and—

LOREN: Vince's parents were shocked. They're very traditional. They got
over it for Vince's sake. They're paying for everything.

SOPHIE: Your fat corporate whore salary could've paid for something.

LOREN: I bought my wedding dress.

SOPHIE: Yeah, Mum showed me. A 70-percent-off 80s reject. Fetching.

LOREN: .
Remember that fight Mum and Azza had? We were playing. We
heard a crash in the kitchen and ran in. Found the table on the floor.
Flipped over. On top of our dinner. That was Azza.

SOPHIE: We don't know that.

LOREN: Instant Jekyll and Hyde on drugs. Aunty snaps.

Imagination: AVENGING AZZA *enters.*

AVENGING AZZA: You public enemy infidel! Get out! I'm going to throw
you to your knees and beat you! Drop you down a well and spit on
you! Cut your stupid impulsive ears off, trample you with camels
until I break your will... This is normal for me, Sophia, a day-to-day
activity.

AVENGING AZZA *exits.*

LOREN: Aunty can't comprehend it. You leaving home and living with
strangers. Being a sneaky arty-farty weirdo with no money who'll
die poor like Dad did.

SOPHIE: Dad did his best.

LOREN: Dad had two daughters. Two weddings he didn't save up for.
Migrants don't do that. Vince's dad's concreting business is worth
a mint.

LOREN *stubs out her smoke, freshens her breath, locks everything
in the glove box.*

SOPHIE: They're not in national dress, are they?

Pause.

LOREN *ululates, and laughs at* SOPHIE*'s reaction.*

AZZA *enters, a cosmopolitan woman in modern dress.*

AZZA: Layla…

SOPHIE: Aunty?

AZZA: Sophia… you look just like her. Your lovely wild hair, the shape of your face…

SOPHIE: Sorry. No Arabic.

AZZA: Do you know about Layla?

SOPHIE: Are you good?

AZZA: It's so good to see you and be here with my nieces who have grown into such beautiful young women.

SOPHIE: Was the flight good?

AZZA: Come, come inside. You look tired. Are you tired? I made your mother wait. *No coffee,* I said. *We're going to wait for Sophia.* She complained, of course, but I insisted.

SOPHIE: Was the weather good when you left Amman?

AZZA: Oh Sophia, you couldn't look more like Layla if you tried.

SOPHIE *is overwhelmed.*

SOPHIE: Ok. I have to go. I'll call you tomorrow.

SOPHIE *exits.*

AZZA: ?

LOREN: She does that.

LOREN *walks towards the house, then turns to Azza.*

[*With an exaggerated gesture*] Come.

LOREN *exits.* AZZA *follows.*

PART TWO

14.

Present: University. SAM *is drinking takeaway coffee.*

SOPHIE: She acted like she was happy to see me.

SAM: So why'd you run?

SOPHIE: It threw me. I'd been so afraid, you know, expecting hell to break loose.

SAM: You have to go back.

SOPHIE: I will. I want to. She wasn't angry at all.

SAM: That's great.

SOPHIE: I think she was happy to see me. Because when she saw me, she didn't see the tantrum-throwing addicted bad person that Mum probably said I was… She could see that I'm actually really humble and quiet.

SAM: Well—

SOPHIE: That I'm a good Arabic girl… who doesn't live at home, which would still shock her… But this is the thing that I think a Western society doesn't understand. It's rare here, but in Jordan, and I imagine it's the same in Italy or Greece or wherever, there's a huge sense of family spirit. We're genuinely close.

SAM: Close?

SOPHIE: It's not that we have to be like this, it's that we are. But here, you're challenged by so many external factors that make you question things, and there's nothing wrong with that, that's good. But here you don't have that same sense of family, you know, you just don't.

SAM: .

> SAM *exits.*

15.

Present: House. SOPHIE *and* LOREN *enter with coffee and sweets.* MARA *is everyone's translator.*

SOPHIE: Is there rigmarole?

LOREN: Just do what Mum does.

> *They serve* MARA *and* AZZA. MARA *indicates her disapproval. They try different things until* MARA *approves, and the conversation can resume.*

AZZA: And Sophia, what do you do?

MARA: Sophia works at the Australian Museum. Don't you?

SOPHIE: ?

MARA: You work at the museum. It's the biggest one in the country. The best one.

AZZA: What do you do there?

MARA: She works on projects. You work on projects.

SOPHIE: Yes, apparently.

AZZA: But what does Sophia do? You said she worked at night. Is she a security guard?

MARA: A what?

AZZA: Security guard.

MARA: Azza, my daughters have done exceptionally well for themselves, without your help. Loren manages company accounts. Sophia works on important projects.

AZZA: At night?

MARA: Yes at night. Why do you work at night?

SOPHIE: I don't know.

MARA: Think.

SOPHIE: Well, obviously we… we share laboratories on a rotating basis.

MARA: Sophia's laboratory is available only after dark. Only a select group of people can access it.

AZZA: In secret?

MARA: Yes.

AZZA: Why?

MARA: Why's your job secret?

SOPHIE: ?

LOREN: Selling pens is so politically sensitive.

MARA: The politics. It's highly sensitive.

AZZA: What politics?

MARA: … Afghanistan.

SOPHIE: ?!

MARA: Sophie leads a team, a team of experts who, they restore priceless treasures damaged by the war.

AZZA: The war fought 10,000 miles away?

MARA: Yes, Azza, obviously, they're in Australia because they're safe.

AZZA: How did they get here?

MARA: How did *you* get here? They crossed the sea.

AZZA: Legally?

MARA: Of course.

AZZA: On the black market, artefacts buy guns. In Syria, right now, they're being dug up and traded for weapons. Sophia, the property you're working with, are you sure it hasn't been looted?

SOPHIE: Mum?

MARA: Your aunt would like more sugar. I trust Sophia as much as I trusted you.

AZZA: It's a fair question.

MARA: Sophia's museum is respected, internationally respected and, they have an agreement. The property will be restored at no cost to Afghanistan and returned with great care when all the fighting stops.

AZZA: Okay, so UNESCO's involved. You should've just said.

SOPHIE: Did she say UNESCO?

MARA: Who are they?

SOPHIE: If there's a war, they go in and protect a country's heritage.

MARA: Good. Your museum works with UNESCO.

SOPHIE: Why?

MARA: They gave you things from Afghanistan to fix.

LOREN: What a clever little checkout chick.

AZZA: Sophia, the artefacts, which era are they from?

SOPHIE: Help.

MARA: What things do you fix? From what time?

AZZA: Afghanistan's been constantly occupied, hasn't it? So its heritage is not just a pile of pots.

SOPHIE: I fix pots.

MARA: Not pots!

SOPHIE: I don't know. Sculptures? Clay sculptures.

MARA: Clay sculptures.

SOPHIE: Greco-Buddhist.

MARA: Greco-Buddhist sculptures.

AZZA: Ah! Sophia, did you know that the destruction of the Bamiyan Buddhas was ordered by the supreme court under the Taliban?

SOPHIE: What?

MARA: Something about the Taliban.

SOPHIE: !

Imagination: SAHIR *enters.*

SAHIR: But Sophia Loren emerged from the rubble.

SOPHIE: Dad?

SAHIR *exits.* SOPHIE *follows.*

16.

Imagination: SOPHIE *walks with* SAHIR.

SOPHIE: It's wall-to-wall Arabic in there, but can I understand the language Mum's lying to her sister in? No. I can't even make hummus.

SAHIR: *Everything you see, I owe to spaghetti.*

SOPHIE: I doubt she ever said that, Dad.

SAHIR: After the war, Italian films were about surviving awful everyday life. The occupation, the damage, the desperate hunger. The people hated those films, they were depressing, but hope rose up from the destruction and rubble.

SOPHIE: Sophia Loren.

SAHIR: The most beautiful woman in history.

SOPHIE: Why'd you name your babies after a sex symbol from Italy? Why didn't you give us, like, Arabic names that probably all mean virtuous devout faithful virgin unto death?

SAHIR: She had a humble beginning. Overcame poverty and sickness. Played modest salt-of-the earth characters.

SOPHIE: In escapist films that made everything shiny and nice.

SAHIR: Yes.

SOPHIE: I know more about a movie star than I know about you. Like, why don't we know why you left Palestine?

17.

Present: SOPHIE *holds the thought from the previous scene.*

Past: Airport. Near the end of the runway, under the flight path, YOUNG MARA *screams at* YOUNG SAHIR.

YOUNG MARA: Sahir, we had a house, my half of my father's house in Amman, in the capital city of a modern Kingdom. Now we have what? A cold and filthy bedsit on the other side of the world. You have work, you have friends at the factory, come home whistling nice happy tunes because you're thinking of that horrible block of wind and cow shit that you expect me to live in. What do I have? A landlady in yelling dresses who blocks the corridor with her bulk and sneers at my cooking. Strangers who get drunk on the steps and live in smelly dark rooms in sin. A husband who grows little sticks in little jars for a little garden that will never smell as sweet as the irises and jasmine you grew for me in Jordan.

YOUNG SAHIR: Land in this land with me.

YOUNG MARA: Arabic!

YOUNG SAHIR: Mara—

YOUNG MARA: Speak Arabic to me!

YOUNG SAHIR: I can't. It cuts my tongue. I choke on the blood. It digs up the dead. English is clean. English is our home now, our future.

YOUNG MARA: Don't do this.

YOUNG SAHIR: Mara, peace is possible here. You're smart, darling, you'll learn English quickly, I'll teach you.

YOUNG MARA: Don't do this, Sahir, don't strand me in my own language, crying all day and unpacking nothing. I have nothing to put away in the home I don't have, the home not built yet for the baby on the way!

YOUNG MARA exits.

YOUNG SAHIR: Mara!

YOUNG SAHIR exits.

A jet screams overhead.

18.

Past: University. STUDENT SAM, *in lab coat, is methodically cataloguing artefacts.*

SOPHIE *enters.*

SOPHIE: It's her fault I'm failing. How can I not fail?

STUDENT SAM: Your exams?

SOPHIE: Whole subjects! I'm still failing subjects from first year.

STUDENT SAM: Brutal.

SOPHIE: How can they not be a write-off with all the yelling that goes on? It's massively bad, it's awful. I'm always in the wrong because I don't prop up the patriarchy in the way she wants me to. It stresses me out and I snap at her and just make it worse.

STUDENT SAM: What happened?

SOPHIE: Mum found my results, found blazing proof that I lie. I do lie. I lie every semester. I really want this degree, but she accuses me, thinks I'm having random orgies with everyone, keeps me locked inside her virgin-whore dichotomy.

STUDENT SAM: Sounds like you passed Women's Studies.

SOPHIE: Got a credit. But Mum saw the other marks, fail fail fail, and went ballistic. I just can't stay within her pre-defined parameters!

STUDENT SAM: You could just move out.

SOPHIE: If I could, I'd defer uni, get a job doing anything, and just get the hell out of there.

STUDENT SAM: Do it.

SOPHIE: I'm not married.

STUDENT SAM: So?

SOPHIE: I've written to my aunt. The one we visited in Amman. If she sponsored me to study or work in Jordan, then maybe I could leave home and escape my mother without getting married first.

STUDENT SAM: You can move to Jordan, but not Glebe?

SOPHIE: Yes.

STUDENT SAM: Don't get it.

SOPHIE: Over there, I'd still be in the family nest. It's woggy logic, but how else can I be single and leave home and assert my autonomy from the dominant order in a way that Mum can accept and tell her friends about?

STUDENT SAM: Have you heard from your aunt yet?

SOPHIE: Not yet. I think she's ignoring me.

STUDENT SAM: Where's the evidence to support that?

SOPHIE: I'm just speculating.

Pause.

SAM *shows* SOPHIE *an artefact.*

SOPHIE: What is it?

STUDENT SAM: Interrogate the artefact.

SOPHIE: Just tell me.

STUDENT SAM: Weight.

SOPHIE: You just weighed it.
STUDENT SAM: Weight.
SOPHIE: I don't know. Less than a kilo? Four hundred grams?
STUDENT SAM: Length.
SOPHIE: It's… as long as my hand.
STUDENT SAM: As wide as your palm.
SOPHIE: Yes.
STUDENT SAM: Distinguishing features.
SOPHIE: Nobs.
STUDENT SAM: Nipples.
SOPHIE: ?
STUDENT SAM: It's a nipple-based incense cup.
SOPHIE: Oh, a cup with—
STUDENT SAM: One on each corner, see?
SOPHIE: What's it for?
STUDENT SAM: The worship of Baal.
SOPHIE: The Old Testament devil.
STUDENT SAM: Or the esteemed Canaanite Lord. Depending.
SOPHIE: Yeah.
STUDENT SAM: Point of view.
SOPHIE: Always.
STUDENT SAM: It's linked, they think, with fertility rites.
SOPHIE: Right.
STUDENT SAM: With offerings…
SOPHIE: Offerings…
STUDENT SAM: To renew the…

   Kiss.

19.

Past: STUDENT SAM *and* SOPHIE *from the previous scene, kissing.*
Present: House. MARA *translates for* AZZA, LOREN *and* SOPHIE.

LOREN: Concrete. Vince works in his dad's business.
MARA: Vince works in construction, in his dad's business. Shopping
   centres, skyscrapers.
LOREN: He's nearly paid his house off.

MARA: He's rich. He'll inherit everything.

LOREN: His parents are paying for the reception. Conca d'Oro Lounge. Doves will fly out of the cake when we... yeah, when we...

AZZA: What?

MARA: She can't wait to cut the cake.

AZZA: Her face didn't say that.

MARA: I know what she said.

AZZA: I know what I saw.

MARA: And I know my daughter.

AZZA: Loren, who *is* Vince? What inspires him? What does your heart say when you see him?

LOREN: ?

MARA: What's Vince like?

LOREN: Soccer, pizza, Xbox.

MARA: No stupid, what's Vince like as a person?

LOREN: He's nice to me.

MARA: Nice?

LOREN: He's strong, physically strong. Lots of lifting.

MARA: What else?

LOREN: He's punctual.

MARA: Punctual?

AZZA: Is Vince too wonderful for words?

MARA: Vince adores her. He's a very attractive man who is protective and reliable and... Loren?

LOREN: Suntanned.

MARA: ?

LOREN: He works outdoors.

MARA: Vince loves being outdoors, in the sun, and travelling to... to sunny destinations.

AZZA: .

MARA: She's just nervous. Wedding jitters.

    LOREN *takes the heat off herself.*

LOREN: Ask Sophia about her flatmate.

    STUDENT SAM *exits.*

We've never met her. She could be living with a child-killing porn star.

AZZA: Something about Sophia?

MARA: Sophia has a flatmate. Samira. She's a good girl. They met at church. Went to uni together.

AZZA: Lovely. What's she like?

MARA: What's Samira like?

SOPHIE: She's bright. Funny and serious. Thoughtful and caring. But not smothery. When she's curious about something, you can't stop her. And she has this amazing gift for bringing history alive.

MARA: She's nice.

AZZA: Her face didn't say.

MARA: For God's sake! I know what she said.

> MARA *exits*.

AZZA: Does Sophie have a boyfriend?

> *Azza exits after* MARA.

20.

Present: Flat. SOPHIE *updates* SAM.

SAM: So, your family on your mum's side—

SOPHIE: They're not money from money, they're money from hard work and intelligence and contacts. Aunty's school, it's the equivalent of SCEGGS. And Mum didn't get married until she was 30-something, remember, because on her side, career was always pushed. Which is why my second cousins haven't all just walked into like, whatever, labourer jobs. They're all bright and career-focused, she said, all studying brilliant things, and all topping their year.

SAM: I can't wait to meet them.

SOPHIE: When?

SAM: Next year. Troy, Ephesus, Petra? You've got cousins over there. That's so cool.

SOPHIE: Second cousins.

SAM: Yeah, who we can connect with. They can show us the city.

SOPHIE: They're not obligated.

SAM: Obviously, but they'll totally want to hang out with us. Exploring Amman, swapping gossip. And they're bright, right? So they'll pick it up. They'll ask you about me.

SOPHIE: You?

SAM: Us. And you can tell them all about our pokey home under the flight path, our desperate longing for a dog, our lack of talent for same-sex salsa.

SOPHIE: But, Sam, things are patched up now, fully reconciled nearly.

SAM: Perfect timing.

SOPHIE: No, seriously, my family's reaction'd be... they'd kill me... it'd kill them.

SAM: Older relos, maybe, but—

SOPHIE: No, my second cousins would—

SAM: They're young and educated and—

SOPHIE: Well, their issues would be things like, hair removal, and *Do you go to nightclubs? Do you get drunk?* But that's it. They're bottled. Their mindset wouldn't expand further than that. If we said anything about, you know...

SAM: Being lesbians?

SOPHIE: Parents would be told. We'd have to take our life in one chunk and cremate it and throw it over a cliff and wipe it out of everyone's mind.

SAM: Or live our lives without them.

SOPHIE: It's not like that in Jordan.

SAM: You don't live in Jordan.

SOPHIE: .

SAM: I've never been a closet case, Sophie.

SOPHIE: You've never *had* to be.

SAM: But, you're loved, I love you, wouldn't your family be thrilled to know that?

SOPHIE: A hundred percent no way in hell.

SAM: Really?

SOPHIE: Really.

SAM: Is such a family worth having?

SOPHIE: My family's been through war and occupation and poverty and—

SAM: Not your mum's side.

SOPHIE: You don't even know them!

SAM: That's right. I have a mother-in-law I haven't met, a sister-in-law whose wedding I wasn't invited to, an aunt-in-law who doesn't even know I exist!

SOPHIE: They're not your in-laws.

SAM: .

SOPHIE: Not *actually*.

> *Pause.*

SAM: Would you marry me? Would you? If I proposed right now, promised to love you forever exactly as you are... what would you do?

21.

Present: House. AZZA *shows photos to* SOPHIE *and* LOREN.

Past: YOUNG SAHIR *calls* YOUNG MARA *from a payphone. He is on the run.*

LOREN: Is that *Mum?*

AZZA: This was their honeymoon.

SOPHIE: Is that the Dead Sea? Mum?

> MARA *nods.*

LOREN: Wow.

SOPHIE: Salt icebergs.

LOREN: Was this your honeymoon?

SOPHIE: That white is blinding.

LOREN: Going somewhere dead after your wedding sounds wrong.

SOPHIE: It's popular.

LOREN: Noosa's better.

SOPHIE: Check out the cossie! You look incredible, Mum.

LOREN: Happy. Actually happy.

AZZA: Does Loren ever smile?

MARA: Why did you bring these?

AZZA: Why haven't they seen them?

SOPHIE: Why haven't we seen these?

AZZA: Remember when you got engaged? Sit with us, Mara. Look how happy you look.

MARA: Look how long it lasted.

LOREN: Oh my God.

SOPHIE: That's me.

LOREN: Your prettier twin.

Doris Younane as Mara, Sheridan Harbridge as Loren, Camilla Ah Kin as Azza and Alice Ansara as Sophie in Griffin Theatre Company's 2014 production. (Photo: Brett Boardman)

SOPHIE: Identical hair.

LOREN: Frizz factory.

SOPHIE: Mum? Is that Layla? Dad's sister?

MARA *snatches the photo out of their hands.*

YOUNG SAHIR: Mara, Layla's dead. Shot in the camp. I've been going to the camp. I'm sorry. I'm walking north. I'm sorry...

Past: YOUNG SAHIR *exits.*

AZZA: Do they know about Layla?

SOPHIE: Can I make some copies?

MARA: No.

MARA *exits.*

22.

Past: University. SOPHIE *and* STUDENT SAM *are studying an artefact, a bull box, by drawing it.*

SOPHIE: Dad said my curls were a gift from his sister, Layla. I'm her spitting image, apparently. She died before I was born. In Palestine. Or Jordan. I don't know. What about your family?

STUDENT SAM: Irish-Scottish Aussie.

SOPHIE: Migrants.

STUDENT SAM: Way back. Potato famine refugees, Calvinist crackpots, we don't know.

SOPHIE: Don't you want to know?

STUDENT SAM: I want to finish this assignment.

SOPHIE: Me too.

They resume drawing, until...

Who do *you* look like?

STUDENT SAM: My dad.

SOPHIE: What does he do?

STUDENT SAM: Drives a truck.

SOPHIE: Where?

STUDENT SAM: Everywhere... We have this thing. Every summer holiday, he takes me on the road with him. Until I turned vegan, we'd live on lamingtons and battered savs. Yeah, gross, but incredible. The pick of the season in the back of the rig. Mangoes, avocados, cherries. I love it. The independence of it. Coming home with Tibooburra dust on your dash.

SOPHIE: Desert dust.

STUDENT SAM: In your clothes, up your nose...

SOPHIE: Hey, our dads both crossed deserts.

STUDENT SAM: Yeah.

SOPHIE: Imagine if they'd met. They might've found something in common.

STUDENT SAM: Maybe. Because a roadhouse, I always thought, if you magnified it by a million, it'd kind of be like what Petra was. A pit stop where travellers on different roads can rest up and trade stories over steak sandwiches.

SOPHIE: Kebabs.

STUDENT SAM: Kebabs.

STUDENT SAM *smiles, and resumes drawing, until...*

SOPHIE: I'm bored!

STUDENT SAM: Why do you think we're drawing?

SOPHIE: Because our lecturer's a douchebag?

STUDENT SAM *holds the bull box under* SOPHIE*'s nose.*

STUDENT SAM: This bull box is made of what?

STUDENT SAM *waits until* SOPHIE *really looks at the artefact.*

SOPHIE: Clay?

STUDENT SAM: Describe the surface.

SOPHIE: Polished, but not super-polished?

STUDENT SAM: All over?

SOPHIE: Yes?

STUDENT SAM: It's polished on the outside, burnished, probably with a tool, right?

SOPHIE: Right.

STUDENT SAM: But inside, those of us who are drawing it can see slight ridges, a rougher texture, marks possibly left by someone's thumbs.

SOPHIE *looks.*

SOPHIE: You're right. You're the shit.

STUDENT SAM *resumes drawing until...*

Bulls are connected to Baal, right?

SAM: .

SOPHIE: Courtney saw Baal. At Pella when she went on that dig. She said she saw him as large as life sitting on the end of her bed carrying a very exotic flowerpot.

SAM: .

SOPHIE: [*mimicking Courtney*] *On a dig, I have all these dreams, vivid dreams, they're practically visitations!*

STUDENT SAM *gives up, and shuts her up with a kiss.*

23.

Present: House. SOPHIE *is showing* AZZA *some drawings.*

AZZA: You drew these?

SOPHIE: This is a pottery theatre ticket. Well, my dodgy drawing of one. Pottery, you know, (mime) clay... hands... make.

AZZA: Make.

SOPHIE: They made clay tickets, sold clay tickets for the theatre.

AZZA: ?

SOPHIE: [*miming*] Comedy, tragedy, Shakespeare, *to be or not to be.* Theatre.

AZZA: Theatre. Theatre, yes.

MARA *enters.*

AZZA: Have you seen Sophia's drawings? Artefacts from Afghanistan.

SOPHIE: No, not Afghanistan. Sorry, should've said, these were found in Jordan.

AZZA: Jordan?

SOPHIE: At Pella. My uni sponsors a dig there.

MARA: Her museum sponsors a dig there.

AZZA: Why is she drawing artefacts from Jordan?

MARA: They're from her previous job. Before her promotion.

AZZA: When?

MARA: Last year.

AZZA: But this is dated this year. See?

MARA: Why are you drawing artefacts from Jordan?

SOPHIE: My uni assignment.
MARA: Not uni. You work at the museum. You work for UNESCO.
SOPHIE: Not this again.
MARA: Don't you?
SOPHIE: No. No, Aunty. No UNESCO. It's not true.
AZZA: No UNESCO?
MARA: Sophia—
SOPHIE: No, Mum. Can we just tell her please, and stop this?

   MARA *exits.*

Aunty... I work in a department store. Some customers treat me like I'm their servant. My supervisor cuts my shifts if I don't gift-wrap in the regulation fashion. My manager wears red polyester shoulder-padded jackets and cuts my shifts if I don't use these hard-sell phoney American techniques which I hate and refuse to use because I respect people's right to shop unharrassed. I earn twenty dollars an hour and loathe every minute of it... But telling you, Aunty, I'm a bit relieved, you know, because, I don't know... I don't like lying to people I adore.

   Pause.

AZZA: No Afghanistan?
SOPHIE: No.
AZZA: Thank you.

24.

Present: Flat. SAM *enters with a packed bag.*

SAM: Dad called.
SOPHIE: Oh.
SAM: Did his usual pitch. *Be my summer offsider, Sam. Camp under the stars, wake up to the sizzle of baked beans and bacon fat...* and we started crapping on about me being a vegan princess and him being a boofy carnivore... and it was mad, you know, that fun between us... and it felt... He makes me feel like I'm a part of his world. And yes, you're not my father, you're my lover, and no, I'm not into smothery clingy joined-at-the hip shit, but... I don't feel like I'm part of your world.
SOPHIE: Are you—?

SAM: I get why you can't be honest about me... But being cut out of your life, even part-time... I need to think about it.

SOPHIE: Is this a break?

SAM: Dad's doing the Darwin run. Up through the desert. I've said no for the last three years... but I love those long hauls.

SOPHIE: Is this a break-up?

SAM: I'll probably be out of range a lot.

> *Kiss.*

I hope the wedding...

> SAM *exits.*

PART THREE

25.

Present: Garage. LOREN *is chain-smoking.*

LOREN: We're having a comedian at our wedding.

SOPHIE: .

LOREN: We saw him at Vince's cousin's nephew's wedding. He sings that yodelling song. Tells jokes. He's funny. Not too expensive.

SOPHIE: .

LOREN: The venue has this new menu. Edible flowers. Every course. We picked banana blossom salad with chicken. Salmon with nasturtium vinaigrette. And two desserts. Vince picked orange mousse in tulip cups. I picked lavender cranberry crisps. Vince wanted Italian. Tiramisu. But Vince—

SOPHIE: Vince Vince fucking Vince! You just, you think you're so entitled to talk about him constantly, even though he's massively rude and arrogant, and doesn't lift a finger, or touch Arabic food. He made Mum make steak and chips!

LOREN: Chickpeas don't agree with him.

SOPHIE: He's come *once* to meet Aunty, once. Takes zilch interest in his new in-law who crossed oceans especially to meet him.

LOREN: He's nearly my husband! *Best wishes on your engagement!* It's fucking lucky I'm not allergic!

SOPHIE: What are you talking about?

LOREN: The flowers.
SOPHIE: What flowers?
LOREN: The waratahs. From Aunty Azza.
SOPHIE: Aunty sent flowers?
LOREN: Wall-to-wall. You can't move in there. They're just gonna die!
SOPHIE: Loren, are you alright?

Imagination: SAHIR *enters.*

SAHIR: The waratah is known to be a very difficult plant.
SOPHIE: Dad?

SAHIR *walks.* SOPHIE *follows.*

26.

Present: House. SOPHIE *is surrounded by flowers.*

Imagination: SAHIR *arranges waratahs in a vase.*

Past: Home. YOUNG MARA *enters with a suitcase and glares at* SAHIR.

SAHIR: My waratah cuttings always died. But then I read up on it. *Take a cutting when the shrub is flush with growth.* So I mixed existing soil with new soil and leaf mulch, then planted the healthiest cutting I could find. In the months ahead, I watered it regularly, kept my eye on the soil so that it never dried out. In time, with care, it bloomed.
SOPHIE: Dad, Sam's surrounded by flowers, too. In a truck on a highway hugged by wildflowers, probably. Because it's started raining in the outback, Dad. Flash floods. Sam's gone, Dad. Sam left me.
YOUNG MARA: I left you, Sahir. I went to Jordan with the girls and left you for good. I wasn't on holiday. I wasn't coming back, but Azza wouldn't help. She sent me and the girls back. That's why I'm back.

YOUNG MARA *throws the waratahs on the floor.*

Bring one more flower into this house, and I promise you, I will turn your garden to stone.

YOUNG MARA *exits.* SAHIR *picks up the waratahs and exits.*

27.

Present: House. SOPHIE *and* LOREN *wait in the lounge room. Hippy music is coming from the kitchen.* AZZA *enters, spreads a sheet of plastic on the floor, then exits.*

SOPHIE: What's the plastic for?

LOREN: .

SOPHIE: Maybe Aunty's hired a stripper, and the plastic's for, you know, whipped cream, as in, woo hoo, happy hen's night.

LOREN: Maybe she wants to behead you.

SOPHIE: .

Maybe she was in the PLO. Maybe she was some sort of operative.

LOREN: Maybe she was the first lady suicide bomber who blew herself up making chastity bomb belts on her kitchen bench.

SOPHIE: Loren. Chill.

LOREN: I am chilled.

    Pause.

SOPHIE: What if it's an Arab thing?

LOREN: What if *what* is?

SOPHIE: You know, messed-up mindsets like… Mum forcing Dad to drive to the airport where she could yell at him hysterically… Aunty flipping over a table full of food—

LOREN: What is this, fucking Family History Month?

    AZZA *enters, stirring a pot.*

AZZA: Loren, next week is your wedding, a joyous occasion, so let's celebrate! Mara!

    MARA *enters.*

Mara, let's pamper your precious daughter. Let's dance, sing and break a couple of chairs, because that's what it's about, before a wedding, being extravagantly happy.

MARA: .

AZZA: Clearly, a foreign concept… Sophia? Loren? The food's ready. Please bring the food in.

SOPHIE: ?

LOREN: ?

MARA: .

AZZA: [*miming*] In the kitchen. Food.

SOPHIE: [*miming*] Food?

AZZA: [*miming*] Bring it in here.

SOPHIE: [*miming*] Go get the food?

AZZA: Please.

> SOPHIE *and* LOREN *exit.* MARA *grabs for the pot.*

MARA: I'll do it.

AZZA: No.

MARA: I'll do it.

AZZA: No.

MARA: Give it to me. We could be sisterly about this. But what do you do? Kick me out of my kitchen. Push the table against the door. Dig around in my cupboards. I had to drink from the garden hose like a dog!

AZZA: Why are your daughters so miserable?

> *From the kitchen,* SOPHIE *and* LOREN *exclaim with amazement and delight.*
>
> *They enter with food.*

SOPHIE: Pavlova!

AZZA: With pomegranates and mint. Wahibe's variation.

MARA: Wahibe?

AZZA: You don't know Wahibe? She sells coffee and sweets at Macarthur Square. I followed my nose. Found a translator I could trust.

LOREN: Pad Thai.

AZZA: *I want to cook up a storm,* I said. *All Australian food.* She wasn't sure what Australian was but, *Azza,* she said, *have a seat, have a coffee. I'll ask my customers.*

SOPHIE: Tiny pies.

LOREN: I love pies.

AZZA: Beef and shiraz.

SOPHIE: This lamb smells super-awesome.

AZZA: Cumin lamb cutlets with grilled peach chutney.

SOPHIE: Pizza!

AZZA: Pide. Peppered fig and ricotta. My signature dish.

LOREN: Can we start?

MARA: No. Don't eat it. Don't touch it. This is my house. I'm the cook. Loren, Sophia, come.

LOREN: But the food's ready.

MARA: It'll be ready when I make it.

SOPHIE: You're kidding, right?

MARA: Come.

LOREN: But Aunty's gone to all this trouble.

MARA: Azza is trouble.

SOPHIE: She's made dinner for us, a feast.

MARA: Don't eat that.

SOPHIE: But, Mum, Aunty's slaved all day. It's rude and pretty crazy to not thank her by enjoying it. I'm not passing this up.

SOPHIE eats. It is delicious.

Oh my God.

MARA: Loren, come.

LOREN: No.

MARA: Come.

LOREN: No. Suffer. You will anyway. You wreck everything.

LOREN eats. It is delicious.

This is amazing.

SOPHIE: These pies…

LOREN: Try the lamb, it's…

SOPHIE: Oh my God.

LOREN: Seriously, it's totally…

SOPHIE: Aunty…

LOREN: … awesome.

SOPHIE: Thank you, this is so…

AZZA understands.

AZZA: Darlings, it's a pleasure. Eat up. Mara. Join us.

MARA: .

SOPHIE notices MARA glaring at AZZA.

SOPHIE: Hey. I've worked out what the plastic's for.

LOREN: What?

SOPHIE: Food fight.

SOPHIE *and* LOREN *laugh.*

AZZA *stirs a pot.*

AZZA: Okay, this is ready. Shall we begin?

SOPHIE: Loren!

LOREN: What?

SOPHIE: That's wax! I'm out of here.

LOREN: Wax?

SOPHIE: You know, for… [*She demonstrates*] It's cultural. It's torture!

AZZA: Loren.

SOPHIE: *You!* She wants *you!*

AZZA: If we were in Jordan, you'd trust us with your beauty.

SOPHIE: It must be a wedding ritual.

AZZA: We'd encircle you, create an salon of pure indulgence, and pamper you until you glowed with our love.

SOPHIE: You're going to be stripped!

AZZA: Some traditions need to be defied, but not this one.

SOPHIE: Blotchy and hobbling and red raw and—

LOREN: How stripped?

SOPHIE: Aunty? [*Miming*] That wax, how far up?

AZZA *gestures up to the eyebrows.*

She's going to denude you! Which, Loren, that's great. I mean, it's so personal and ethnically meaningful and… Oh my God! This is so funny. She's the stripper! Aunty's the stripper!

SOPHIE *laughs.* LOREN *sees the joke and laughs too.*

AZZA: Shall we begin?

LOREN *cracks a lame joke.*

LOREN: No skin off my nose.

She laughs and steps onto the plastic.

AZZA: Sophia?

SOPHIE: Me?

AZZA: Yes.

SOPHIE: On there?

AZZA: Yes.

SOPHIE: No way.

LOREN: But it's so *ethnically meaningful.*
SOPHIE: Shut up.
LOREN: Come on.

With dread, SOPHIE *steps onto the plastic.*

The girls brace themselves. AZZA *applies wax to* LOREN. *The effect is surprisingly soothing.*

SOPHIE: Is it revolting?
LOREN: …
SOPHIE: It's gross, right?
LOREN: …
SOPHIE: Sticky and repulsive and—
LOREN: No… it's weird… but good weird… like a kind of second skin.

AZZA *tears a strip off* LOREN*'s leg.* LOREN *yelps. They laugh.*

Stripping and eating and laughing continue, ad-libbed, without any need of an interpreter.

MARA *exits.*

28.

Present: House. Alone on the patio, MARA *overhears* SOPHIE *and* LOREN *talking and laughing.*

SOPHIE: [*off*] My skin is burnt! It's burning!
LOREN: [*off*] I've got serious skin damage.
SOPHIE: [*off*] My pores are panicking. I'll probably get some nasty bacteria.
LOREN: [*off*] Or warts. Warts grow from injured skin.
SOPHIE: [*off*] Shit. I'm so gonna be covered in them.

AZZA *enters with a plate of food.*

AZZA: Lovely night.
MARA: .
AZZA: You should eat.
MARA: .
AZZA: Can I show you something?

AZZA *takes out a letter and reads some of it to* MARA.

AZZA: ... *I'm desperate to get to Jordan... to sip coffee at Petra in the half-darkness until the sun hits the cliffs... If I could come and live with you... if you could introduce me to anyone in antiquities, I might be able to set myself up... I really want to be good at something I love...*

MARA: Sophia wrote to you?

AZZA: Five years ago.

MARA: About living with you?

AZZA: About work. Did you translate it for her?

MARA: She didn't tell me about this.

> *Pause.*

AZZA: Did she get my reply?

MARA: .

AZZA: I'd look after Sophia. Arrange meetings, interviews, work experience.

MARA: .

AZZA: It's a standing offer. No hurry. No conditions. No need for her to worry about the cost of anything... Will you tell her? Mara? If she's still interested, I'm offering to take Sophia to Jordan.

> *Pause.*

MARA: She doesn't speak Arabic.

AZZA: Not at the moment.

> *Pause.*

MARA: Sophia.

> SOPHIA *enters, followed by* LOREN.

MARA: You wrote to Azza?

SOPHIE: Once.

MARA: You wrote to my sister?

SOPHIE: Only about work.

> *Pause.*

MARA: Azza is willing to take you to Jordan.

LOREN: What?

MARA: She will look after you. Arrange meetings, interviews, work experience. She'll pay for everything you need.

SOPHIE: Really?

MARA: You'd have to work hard.

SOPHIE: I would. I'd work like a dog. When can I go? Not in summer. Their summers are stifling. They usually get cholera. Do they still get cholera. Where would I live? Would people really give me a job? Aunty, oh my God, this is so—

AZZA *kisses* SOPHIE, *and exits.*

Pause.

MARA: There's a condition.

SOPHIE: … Okay.

MARA: You have no Arabic.

SOPHIE: I'll take classes, those intensive ones.

MARA: I'll teach you.

SOPHIE: No, there's a community college that—

MARA: No. Azza wants me to teach you. She insists.

SOPHIE: That you teach me?

MARA: At home. You'll move home and learn from me, until your Arabic is not an embarrassment. Azza insists.

SOPHIE: But that could take years. I have flatmate obligations, a lease and—

MARA: Azza insists. That's the offer. You're free to say no.

MARA *exits.*

Pause.

LOREN: You'll have to get naked.

SOPHIE: What?

LOREN: In Jordan. You'll probably massage Aunty, then she'll do you.

SOPHIE: You think so?

LOREN: You'll have to go with tradition.

SOPHIE: Some of the time, otherwise I'll—

LOREN: Visit relatives.

SOPHIE: Sure, who don't know me, out of respect and—

LOREN: Get checked out.

SOPHIE: Well, obviously they're going to be curious. Who's that Australian girl living with Azza?

LOREN: She'd be your mum over there.

SOPHIE: Not that I really need—

LOREN: Introducing you. Spreading the word.

SOPHIE: Like, not nasty word.

LOREN: Sophia's single.

SOPHIE: An archaeologist.

LOREN: Even if you looked like a dog, that'd be it.

SOPHIE: What would be it?

LOREN: If you came across in the remotest way nice—

SOPHIE: Which I would.

LOREN: Like a nice person, then yeah.

SOPHIE: Yeah?

LOREN: Cousins, nephews, male friends who want a wife—

SOPHIE: Wife!

LOREN: Queuing up. Their mothers on the phone. *Hello Azza?*

> *Imagination:* AVENGING AZZA *enters.*

AVENGING AZZA: Hello?

LOREN: *Can my husband and 16 children come with me to visit?*

AVENGING AZZA: Why?

LOREN: *Hairy Toothless Tarek is interested.*

AVENGING AZZA: Sophie! Put some clothes on! Hairy Toothless Tarek is interested!

SOPHIE: No way.

LOREN: The whole tribe will come over. Check you out over coffee and sweets.

SOPHIE: No.

AVENGING AZZA: Do you like him, Sophia? Do you like the look of him, Sophia?

SOPHIE: No. I'm free to say no. I'm going there to work.

LOREN: At first.

SOPHIE: That's the offer.

LOREN: That's what you think.

SOPHIE: … You think there's a plan?

LOREN: A plot.

AVENGING AZZA: Hello. Is this Hairy Toothless Tarek's mother? This is Azza. Sophia's aunty. She is very interested in Hairy Toothless

Tarek... Can I come now and visit?... Good. Let's discuss the engagement, and the bride price.

Imagination: AVENGING AZZA *exits.*

SOPHIE: What plot?
LOREN: To arrange you, you idiot. Restore Mum's honour. Make you respectable behind your back.

LOREN *exits.*

PART FOUR

29.

Present: House. SOPHIE *is on the patio.*

Past: House. MARA *is alone. A compacter can be heard in the backyard.* SAHIR *enters.*

MARA: They measured out the area for the slab. Started digging. Excavating. That's what they called it. They dug down, removed rocks and roots, then got this machine to punch the dirt flat.

SAHIR *looks out the back door into the yard.*

When they finish, I have to hose the dirt. That way, tomorrow, when they pour the concrete, it won't dry out too quickly and crack.

The compacting sound stops.

SAHIR: My garden.
MARA: Patio.
SAHIR: Why?
MARA: I warned you.
SAHIR: Why?

MARA *exits.*

Pause.

SOPHIE: Dad. Aunty might be plotting to arrange me.

Pause.

SAHIR: Look. The kebab van at the petrol station's still open. Let's go.

SAHIR *walks.*

30.

Imagination: House. AVENGING AZZA *enters with a very exotic flowerpot.*

AVENGING AZZA: Of course it's a plot. All of a sudden I'm nice to you? Work it out. Here. Have a present.

SOPHIE: What is it?

AVENGING AZZA: A very exotic flowerpot.

SOPHIE: Didn't Courtney see Baal carrying a very exotic flowerpot?

AVENGING AZZA: Yes. He's waiting. Hurry up.

SOPHIE: Baal is waiting?

AVENGING AZZA: Baal's your fiancé. Now stop being a checkout chick loser prostitute, and come.

> AVENGING AZZA *exits.*

31.

Present: House. SOPHIE *is alone.* LOREN *enters.*

Past: Amman Citadel. YOUNG MARA *and* YOUNG SAHIR *are in love.*

LOREN: Sophia. Mum's gone.

SOPHIE: What?

LOREN: Mum's missing.

SOPHIE: Did I fall asleep?

LOREN: Sophia! I don't know where Mum is!

SOPHIE: Okay. It's okay. Does she normally go—?

LOREN: No.

SOPHIE: But where could, is there a place where—?

LOREN: She stays home.

SOPHIE: The mall maybe?

LOREN: She never goes out, Sophia. Only when I drive her.

SOPHIE: But a friend, an old bingo friend?

LOREN: She cut ties.

SOPHIE: With everyone?

LOREN: Yes.

SOPHIE: Alright. Maybe she just—

LOREN: An accident? Call the police.

SOPHIE: Wait, what happened? Did something happen?

LOREN: No. I don't know. I've looked everywhere, in every room, outside, in the garage. It's like she just got up and flew—

Pause.

BOTH: Airport!

YOUNG MARA: I love it up here. The feeling up here.

YOUNG SAHIR: I love the way you look up here.

YOUNG MARA: Dusty.

YOUNG SAHIR: Framed by the sky, above our lookout.

YOUNG MARA: What do you feel up here?

YOUNG SAHIR: Love.

YOUNG MARA: And?

YOUNG SAHIR: More love.

YOUNG MARA: [*shouting to the world*] I love Sahir! When I walk around these walls, when I see all of Amman, ancient and new, all swept together into one bustling vastness… see people stuck in traffic, entering hotels and cafes and mosques… think of my students flying kites across gravel that has Stone Age blood, sweat and tears in it… see our children-to-be smiling in your beautiful quiet eyes… standing here in the Citadel among all this… I can breathe.

LOREN: She left without yelling. In blazing silence. That's heaps worse than being screamed at because—

SOPHIE: Loren. One of us should stay. If Mum comes back, and no one's here—

LOREN: Right. Yep.

SOPHIE: Goose chase.

LOREN: Stupid. You stay with Aunty. If Mum turns up, call me immediately, okay? I'll come straight back.

SOPHIE: Will you be—

LOREN: Yes.

LOREN *exits.*

Past: YOUNG MARA *shows* YOUNG SAHIR *the Citadel Inscription.*

YOUNG MARA: Have you read this?

YOUNG SAHIR: What is it?

YOUNG MARA: The Citadel Inscription. A tiny stone tablet inscribed with the promise of a god.

YOUNG SAHIR: With words of weight.

YOUNG MARA: Yes.

YOUNG SAHIR: Maybe that's why it broke.

YOUNG MARA: Maybe… Read it to me.

YOUNG SAHIR: Why?

YOUNG MARA: I want to hear your voice restore the fragments of this promise.

YOUNG SAHIR: *… and amidst its columns the just will reside …*
… there will hang from its door an ornament …
… will be offered within its portico …
… and safety …
peace to you and peace

> YOUNG SAHIR *adds his own ending.*

to our children-to-be
to your home with me
peace

> *Kiss.*

YOUNG MARA: Promise me that you'll stop going to the camp.

YOUNG SAHIR: .

YOUNG MARA: I don't want you hurt.

YOUNG SAHIR: … I promise.

32.

Imagination: Outback. SAHIR *is at a roadhouse.*

Present: House. SOPHIE *is trying to reach* SAM *by phone.*

SOPHIE: Dad… Sam's camping under the stars… But I feel dumped beside a highway, deafened by monster trucks roaring past and ripping me to bits. Sam being out of range feels just like that.

> *Imagination:* TRUCKIE SAM *enters with a kebab.*

TRUCKIE SAM: Sahir, aren't you supposed to be dead?

> SAHIR *takes the kebab and has a bite.*

SAHIR: Excellent kebab.

TRUCKIE SAM: The cook's granddad was Turkish.

They share the kebab and trade stories.

SAHIR: Where are we?

TRUCKIE SAM: Little Afghanistan. Marree actually. But they called it that because cameleers crossing the desert would stop here to rest… until trucks made them redundant.

SAHIR: Sophia said it rained.

TRUCKIE SAM: Thunderstorms. Flash floods. It all drained into Lake Eyre, then summoned up the pelicans and whistling ducks.

SAHIR: And the wildflowers?

TRUCKIE SAM: All the way to the horizon. Sturt's Desert Peas especially. It felt like driving through endless streamers of red and green.

SAHIR: Did you know the Sturt's Desert Pea is a ditch-dwelling plant?

TRUCKIE SAM: Really?

SAHIR: That way, the rain trickles towards them. They sprout quickly, flower quickly, then die quickly… leaving seeds dormant until the next downpour.

TRUCKIE SAM: Petra channelled rain, too. The Nabataeans engineered this system of pipes and reservoirs, so in the middle of the desert, they could grow a lush garden refuge. A *paradeisoi*. A Paradise on Earth.

SAHIR: I had a garden. Nothing but natives.

TRUCKIE SAM: What happened?

SAHIR: It was buried under concrete.

TRUCKIE SAM: … Is that why you walk?

SAHIR: Why do you drive a truck?

TRUCKIE SAM: Well, flying up a highway, singing your head off, with the landscape constantly changing all around you, it's…

SAHIR: Freedom.

TRUCKIE SAM: Yes.

SAHIR: That's why I walk.

TRUCKIE SAM: … Sahir. Archaeologically, your garden's still there. Traces of it still exist. Seeds, minerals, pollen.

SAHIR: It was a gift for my sister Layla.

TRUCKIE SAM: It's still there.

SAHIR: Good, Sam. Good.

33.

Imagination: AVENGING AZZA *enters and rolls out a magic carpet.*

SOPHIE: What's that?

AVENGING AZZA: Hop on.

They do.

AVENGING AZZA: I will hand you to Baal as a divine gift.

SOPHIE: I thought you engaged me to Hairy Toothless Tarek.

AVENGING AZZA: That's Baal's alias.

SOPHIE: My fiancé needs an alias?

AVENGING AZZA: Donkey pervert! Look where you're going!

SOPHIE: What does Baal do?

AVENGING AZZA: Insurance jobs. Torching things. The odd bit of pillage. His father built the business up from nothing. When you meet him, sign the marriage contract without persuasion, or we will feed your eyes to falcons, which tend to spoil the photos, so please don't. Hurry up, you hyena-headed slut!

SOPHIE: When did I consent?

AVENGING AZZA: I did.

SOPHIE: To what exactly?

AVENGING AZZA: Cooking him traditional delicacies, folk dancing on demand, being the vessel for his perpetual lineage… and never forgetting that chickpeas don't agree with him. Oh, and not mentioning that he's a false god. It's a touchy subject… Put your motherfucking foot down!

SOPHIE: I have to folk dance for a false god?

AVENGING AZZA: Yes, and if Baal says *squat down and give birth behind that bush,* you squat down and do it. Which reminds me, he likes to relax by having sex with his goat. Offer to hold it for him. It can get a bit frisky… See that? No blinker! Brain of a dead camel's dick!

SOPHIE: I don't want to.

AVENGING AZZA: Don't want to what?

SOPHIE: Hold his goat.

AVENGING AZZA: You have to. It's in the contract.

SOPHIE: Which isn't signed yet.

AVENGING AZZA: Darling, Baal is the king of calamity. If you displease him, he will crush your spirit and unleash wave upon wave of destruction.

SOPHIE: I'm going home.

AVENGING AZZA: What are you saying?

SOPHIE: Baal can hold his own goat.

AVENGING AZZA: Sophia! Don't do this. We can't take you back. We've already spent the bride price!

SOPHIE: Stop it! Stop it! I'm going home.

> SOPHIE *jumps off the magic carpet.*

PART FIVE

34.

Imagination: Garage. SOPHIE *notices* TRUCKIE SAM *waiting with a book.*

SOPHIE: Sam… How long have you been waiting?

TRUCKIE SAM: Three years.

> *Pause.*

SOPHIE: If we met now, things'd be different.

TRUCKIE SAM: How?

SOPHIE: I wouldn't be crushed at Christmas.

TRUCKIE SAM: What would you be?

SOPHIE: I'd be with you.

> *Pause.*

> TRUCKIE SAM *indicates the book.*

TRUCKIE SAM: Weight?

SOPHIE: What?

TRUCKIE SAM: Interrogate the artefact. The weight.

SOPHIE: A few hundred grams.

TRUCKIE SAM: Size?

SOPHIE: As long as my hand.

TRUCKIE SAM: Materials?

SOPHIE: Paper, yellowish and brittle. The spine shows wear and tear. Stitching is missing. The language is... Arabic.

TRUCKIE SAM: Are you sure?

SOPHIE: I'll get that verified.... The cover is cardboard, torn, and illustrated... a girl looking up at a smiling cat... *Alice in Wonderland.*

TRUCKIE SAM: You assume.

SOPHIE: Yes, but there's other illustrations scattered... not scattered, printed at intervals... See? The Rabbit, the Hatter, the Queen of Hearts... It's an Arabic Alice... Where did you get this?

TRUCKIE SAM: Interrogate the artefact.

SOPHIE: Tell me.

TRUCKIE SAM: The find-context was...?

SOPHIE: Just tell me.

TRUCKIE SAM: Look harder.

SOPHIE *examines the book, and finds a strip of cellophane.*

SOPHIE: Cellophane. One of those strips that you tear off packaging around tampons or CDs or... smokes. Was this... This was in the glovebox... the glovebox in Dad's car.

Pause.

TRUCKIE SAM: Your aunt is coming.

TRUCKIE SAM *exits.*

35.

Present: Garage. SOPHIE *holds the book from the previous scene.* AZZA *enters, carrying a box of photographs. She sits on the ground and gestures for* SOPHIE *to do the same.* AZZA *places the box between them and opens it. She lifts out something bundled in a scarf and places it on top of the box. She speaks carefully in the little English she knows. Past: Jordan.* YOUNG SAHIR *calls* YOUNG MARA. *He is on the run.*

AZZA: Layla.
　　　Jenin.
　　　West Bank.
　　　Refugee Camp.

YOUNG SAHIR: Mara

Layla's dead.
She was killed in the camp.
YOUNG MARA: What?
AZZA: Layla.
Friend.
Sahir sister.
Sahir look Mara.
Love love love.
YOUNG MARA: What happened?
AZZA: Layla.
Teacher.
Refugee camp.
YOUNG SAHIR: A gunman on a motorbike.
Five or six shots.
The whites of her eyes.
Her body dropped.
Her book.
I caught it.
AZZA: Camp.
Children.
Bad life.
See bad.
Cry cry cry.
YOUNG SAHIR: She was lying on the road.
Bent back legs.
The blood.
Keep breathing.
Keep breathing.
YOUNG MARA: Are you hurt?
AZZA: Layla think.
Theatre.
Story.
Children.
Happy.
Alicia…
Alicia…

SOPHIE *shows her the book.*

SOPHIE: *Alice In Wonderland.*

> AZZA *is surprised.*

> SOPHIE *gives her the book, which she holds with great care.*

YOUNG SAHIR: In the ambulance.
I hold her hands.
Hold her book.
Hold on.

YOUNG MARA: Where are you?

AZZA: Layla think.
Theatre.
New story.
Queen make Alice wedding.
Alice think no.
Bad wedding.
No love love love.

YOUNG SAHIR: Beside her.
I watched her die.

AZZA: Alice think free.
Children think free.
Layla think free.

Man.
Palestine man.
Gun.
Blood blood blood.
Layla die.

YOUNG SAHIR: In the ambulance.
Her last breath.
Stop!
At the checkpoint
I jumped out—
watched the ambulance drive away.

YOUNG MARA: Where are you?

YOUNG SAHIR: I'm walking north.

AZZA: Sahir see Layla die.
Sahir go Lebanon.

No come back.

No no come back.

YOUNG MARA: You promised not to go to the camp!

You promised me!

YOUNG SAHIR: A Palestinian pulled the trigger.

My people are killing my people.

The gunman said I'd be next.

I'm walking north to Lebanon.

YOUNG SAHIR *exits.*

YOUNG MARA: No!

YOUNG MARA *exits.*

AZZA: Layla die.

Azza go house.

Take. [*Referring to bundle*]

Give Sahir.

No give.

Sahir die.

Give Sophia.

AZZA *unwraps the bundle and holds up an old key.*

AZZA: Layla Sahir.

Father Mother.

SOPHIE: My grandparents…

AZZA: Palestine.

Jenin.

Refugee.

Run.

SOPHIE: My grandparents fled.

AZZA: House.

SOPHIE: This key is from their house.

AZZA: Palestine house. Nakba.

SOPHIE: This is key to the house my grandparents were driven from.

The Nakba.

AZZA: Take.

Sophia take.

Sophia love.

AZZA *gives* SOPHIE *the key.* SOPHIE *kisses* AZZA *on both cheeks, according to Jordanian custom.*

SOPHIE: Thank you.

Offstage, MARA *and* LOREN *start yelling.*

36.

Present: House. MARA *is yelling at* LOREN. SOPHIE *and* AZZA *try to intervene.*

LOREN: I don't love him. I'm sorry.

AZZA: What happened?

MARA: The wedding is off.

SOPHIE: What's wrong?

LOREN: I cancelled the wedding.

MARA: She told Vince. She told his parents. She didn't tell me!

LOREN: I knew you'd be like this!

SOPHIE: When did you tell her?

LOREN: I didn't. Vince's mum called about the dresses. She went to their place. Bashed on their door like a maniac.

MARA: They cried. They were disgraced!

LOREN: They weren't. They've been kind to me, and concerned, and supportive because I honestly don't want to make two lives miserable.

SOPHIE: Loren, that was really brave.

MARA: That was stupid!

AZZA: Don't yell at them.

MARA: Shut up!

AZZA: Mara, I know you're angry, but—

MARA: She doesn't love Vince. She doesn't love him. She doesn't know the freedom that gives her. Loren, call Vince.

LOREN: No.

MARA: Call him. Marry him.

LOREN: I don't love him!

MARA: Forget love. With love, he can sway you.

AZZA: Mara, stop, your daughter's upset.

MARA: My daughter is stupid. Loren, it'll work, it'll work better!

Sheridan Harbridge as Loren, Doris Younane as Mara and Alice Ansara as Sophie in Griffin Theatre Company's 2014 production. (Photo: Brett Boardman)

SOPHIE: Mum—

MARA: Shut up! Call Vince! Call him!

AZZA quickly bundles SOPHIE *and* LOREN *out of the room.*

AZZA: Go. It's okay. Go.

LOREN: Vince's parents lost their deposit on the Conca D'Oro lounge, mum, and they didn't even bring it up!

LOREN *and* SOPHIE *exit.*

37.

Present: House. MARA *and* AZZA *have it out.*

MARA: Loren is making a mistake, but what do you do? Take her side. What about my side? What about helping me for once? Standing by me?

AZZA: I do—

MARA: Really Azza? Really? If you did, I wouldn't be in this country.

AZZA: What?

MARA: You knew Sahir was going to Jenin. You didn't stop him. You didn't tell me.

AZZA: I didn't—

MARA: He asked you for books. What did you think he was doing?

AZZA: I didn't ask him.

MARA: You knew it was dangerous. You knew Layla had received death threats.

AZZA: Mara, I lost my best friend. I lost Sahir to another country. I lost you, my sister, my only family, the chance to see those girls grow up.

MARA: I lost everything! … When Sahir ended up in Australia, I begged him, come back to me, come back to Amman, to our beautiful life… I begged for two years… until I couldn't live another minute without him… But when I arrived in Sydney, found him speaking English, ignoring my Arabic, even our invented little love words, I died. When he built me a cockroach box in a paddock, left me in a suburb with other dumped mothers, I died. When he stopped growing irises for me, looked at me with blank eyes, I went to you in tears for help but you—

AZZA: You abducted your kids.

MARA: I came home to Jordan.

AZZA: You ran away.

MARA: I ran to my sister for help.

AZZA: Did Sahir know? Did the kids? They didn't. That's abduction, Mara. You would have been extradited. Deported.

MARA: You turned us away.

AZZA: You had to face facts. Go back, tell Sahir, get a divorce, arrange custody. He was a good man who did his best. The least you could have done was be honest.

MARA: How could you not help me?

AZZA: You think I enjoyed watching your plane disappear?

MARA: He lied to me.

AZZA: He loved his sister. He believed in her work.

MARA: I didn't marry this.

AZZA: You were ambushed by history. Most people are, but most people don't sit down and rot in their own self pity.

MARA: Get out!

Pause.

AZZA: You'll lose Loren, you'll lose Sophia…

AZZA *exits.*

38.

Present: Flat. SOPHIE *and* LOREN *enter.* LOREN *has a suitcase.* SAM *appears during the scene but is not noticed until she speaks.*

SOPHIE: Um, it's small.

LOREN: Good location.

SOPHIE: Noisy.

LOREN: But getting to the city, it's so—

SOPHIE: Convenient.

LOREN: So close and—

SOPHIE: You get used to the planes.

LOREN: But that café you've got next door—

SOPHIE: It makes these evil chocolate-bottomed cheesecake muffin things. We can go later.

LOREN: Great.

SOPHIE: Sit. Have a seat. The park's a dog park. Friendly people. I go there sometimes for a pat.

LOREN: You pat people.

SOPHIE: Dogs.

LOREN: Joke.

SOPHIE: I know.

Pause.

LOREN: So is Samira—?

SOPHIE: This is the kitchen. Some of the other flats look out on brick walls, but this flat has this frangipani tree outside, so it doesn't feel so—

LOREN: That's your bedroom?

SOPHIE: Sorry, messy.

LOREN: It fucking was, wasn't it?

SOPHIE: … You can stay.

LOREN: Thanks.

SOPHIE: Stay as long as—

They hug, awkwardly, probably for the first time in their lives.

LOREN: Um…

SOPHIE: I'll make us a cup of—

LOREN: Where does…?

SOPHIE: I think there's milk that's not off yet.

LOREN: There's one bedroom.

SOPHIE: Fortunately, yeah, it's on the sunny side, so—

LOREN: Two beds or one?

SAM: One.

SOPHIE *ecstatically hurls herself at* SAM, *kissing her and welcoming her home.* LOREN *waits awkwardly.* SOPHIE *eventually remembers* LOREN.

SOPHIE: Loren… I'd like you to meet Sam. I'd like you to like Sam. Because I like Sam a lot. Actually, I love Sam. I love Sam, and I'm ridiculously glad you're back!

SAM: Hi.

LOREN: Hi.

SAM: Cup of tea?

LOREN: Yep.

> LOREN *exits into the kitchen.* SAM *follows.*

39.

Present: Flat. SOPHIE *prepares for the evening.*

Imagination: SAHIR *enters and smiles at* SOPHIE. *He removes a picture from a hook on the wall. He looks proudly at Sophie, then exits.*

SOPHIE *hangs the Nakba key on the hook. She takes out a notebook and practices the pronunciation of some Arabic vocabulary.*

SOPHIE: … *bit tawfiq… ahlan wa sahlan… marhaba…*

> LOREN *enters.*

LOREN: Sorry, the babba ghanoush is a bit oily.

SOPHIE: Shouldn't I cook?

LOREN: You can't cook.

SOPHIE: But you're the guest.

LOREN: Just eat your ghanoush.

SOPHIE: Mum sent my letter back.

> *Recent past:* MARA *enters, reading and writing on a letter.*

LOREN: You wrote to Mum?

SOPHIE: Three sentences. Didn't I tell you?

MARA: *I pat the park on the dog.*

SOPHIE: I sent three basic sentences in baby-step Arabic.

MARA: *I have cake for eat the café.*

SOPHIE: She sent it back.

LOREN: Typical of her to reject it.

SOPHIE: No, she corrected it.

MARA: *Me bus city tomorrow took.*

> MARA *laughs to herself, and exits.*

SOPHIE: Look. In red pen. I expected a scathing rant, but I opened it and nothing, nothing furious, just fixed-up grammar.

LOREN: … Should we ring her?

SOPHIE: Do you want to?

LOREN: Not particularly.

SAM *enters, dressing, and pinches some dip.*

SAM: What time's your date?

LOREN: Got to leave in an hour. What'll I wear?

SAM: I bought a new pencil skirt. Might fit.

SOPHIE: Blue though.

LOREN: Don't do blue. Thanks anyway. Where you going?

SAM: Queer Film Festival's on.

SAM *exits.*

LOREN: Not joining her?

SOPHIE: Not tonight. Got Arabic vowels to drill. Just can't get the hang of them.

LOREN: Do it.

SOPHIE: … *ahlan wa sahlan…*

LOREN: Nuh, shit, do it again.

SOPHIE: … *ahlan wa sahlan…*

LOREN: You'll be fine once you're over there, amongst it all, in Jordan.

LOREN *exits.*

SOPHIE: You think so?

LOREN: [*off*] Know so.

Imagination: SAHIR *enters with flowers. He places them on the ground at the front door.*

SAHIR: *Peace to you and peace.*

He smiles at SOPHIE.

SAHIR: *Peace.*

He exits. SOPHIE *resumes her practice.*

SOPHIE: … *bit tawfiq… ahlan wa sahlan… marhaba…*

THE END

ALSO AVAILABLE
FROM CURRENCY PRESS

THE HANGING
Angela Betzien

Three teenage schoolgirls go missing in Melbourne's hinterland. The clock is ticking, the search is on. One of the girls turns up days later. Confused and unkempt, she has no apparent memory of what happened and where her friends are. Sound familiar? *The Hanging* is a gripping thriller that questions the frequently-occurring spectre of the missing girl in the Australian bush. Its mystery is a postmodern study of social panic and what lies hidden, just out of reach.

ISBN 9781760620509, also available as an ebook

LIGHTEN UP
Nicholas Brown and Sam McCool

John Green is an Anglo-Indian Australian actor who dreams of being cast in his favourite TV soap, Bondi Parade. The problem is, his coloured contacts can't hide the fact that his skin is more brown than white. Meanwhile, his skin-bleached mum is determined for him to procreate with a blonde, white Aussie woman in order to rid the family of any sign of their ethnic heritage. All hell breaks loose when John falls in love with an Indigenous woman called Sandy. This very funny play by actor (and Bollywood leading-man) Nicholas Brown and comedian Sam McCool tells a universal tale of identity, cultural assimilation and bleaching your bits.

ISBN 9781760620288, also available as an ebook

STRANGERS IN BETWEEN / HOLDING THE MAN
Tommy Murphy

In *Strangers in Between*, Shane has fled his family and is seeking refuge in Kings Cross. He meets two strangers: the ultra-urban Will, who offers brotherhood, sex and something unexpected; and Peter, a fifty-year-old gay man whose mother is dying in a nursing home. Shane grapples to reconcile himself with events from his past. But how can he move on when he can't even use laundry powder?

Holding the Man is based on Timothy Conigrave's celebrated memoir of the same name which won the 1995 UN Human Rights Award for Non-Fiction and was voted one of Australia's top 100 most favourite books. Tommy Murphy's stage adaptation faithfully captures the book's heart-wrenchingly honest portrayal of a fifteen-year relationship.

ISBN 9780868197968, also available as separate ebooks

MICHAEL SWORDFISH
Lachlan Philpott

What would happen if someone you knew disappeared? But who is Michael Swordfish? And who knows where he's gone? For two years award-winning playwright Lachlan Philpott collaborated with students from Newington College, Sydney, to bring their voices and worlds to life. *Michael Swordfish* is the exciting product of this collaboration: a play that traverses the tumultuous landscape of the teenage experience with a sober truth and darkly comic voice.

ISBN 9781760620837, also available as an ebook

SHAFANA AND AUNT SARRINAH
Alana Valentine

At the heart of this play is the relationship between an aunt and her niece. Both devout Muslims, the younger woman wants to put on a headscarf, the older woman tries to dissuade her. For Aunt Sarrinah, the hijab represents a world from which she has escaped; for her niece, Shafana, it is personal statement of renewed faith. Alana Valentine has written 'a quietly insightful intervention that portrays what media headlines never can; the multiple meanings of the headscarf for Muslim women'.

ISBN 9780868198828, also available as an ebook